NINE CENTURIES AT COPPED HALL

by Sylvia Keith

This book is dedicated to the Sunday morning volunteers from the Friends of the Copped Hall Trust in admiration for their hard work and enthusiastic support of the Copped Hall Trust.

ISBN
978-0-9544116-1-9

First Published in 2007 by S & J.A.Keith

Printed in Great Britain by
Metloc Printers Limited
Loughton, Essex

ACKNOWLEDGEMENTS

The author acknowledges with wholehearted admiration the seminal research carried out by the late Raymond Cassidy and Alan Cox into the history of Copped Hall, without which the subject matter would have been difficult to assemble.

Much of the research and writing on the Timeline was done by Kay Ross, who generously allowed the Friends to use her work. Other contributors to the Timeline were Denys Favre, John and Margaret Gervis, Georgina Green, Nicola Munday and Kay Rush as well as many other Friends of the Copped Hall Trust and the descendants of those who lived and worked at the Hall.

Original illustrations for the front and back covers were contributed by James A. Keith ARPS who also planned the layout of them. Other pictures are by courtesy of Country Life Picture Library, Lord Petre, English Heritage, Peter Dalton, W.R.Conolly and Peter Huggins for his 1066 map.

I also acknowledge the use of the archives of the Essex Record Office and their help.

In this expanded version I am grateful to Pat Styles for her information about the walled garden, Nicola Munday for her research into the 1758 house, Tina Holloway for her archaeological studies and to Wendy Brimble and Patricia Levi for their permission to use an extract from their father's book.

I have taken great care to seek permission to use all the illustrations and written material. However, if I have omitted to obtain that permission from anybody, then I apologise and ask that the copyright holder advises me.

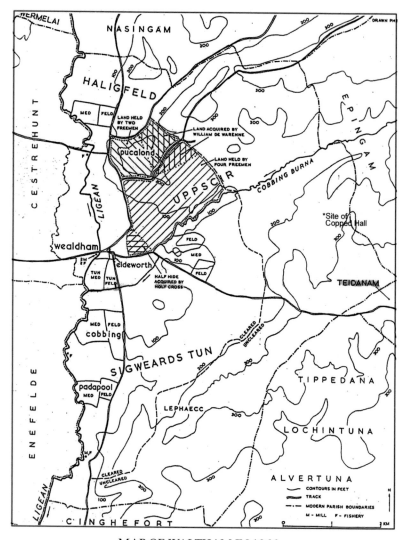

MAP OF WALTHAM IN 1066

by Peter Huggins

PREFACE

The history of Copped Hall may be divided into four phases. The first part is the time from the Norman Conquest up until the building of the Tudor mansion, then the Heneages, Cranfields and Conyers who lived in the Tudor house, thirdly the Georgian mansion and the Conyers and Wythes families who lived there, and lastly what has happened to the site since the fire in 1917 and the more recent moves to preserve and use it for the benefit of the local community.

The name Copped Hall or 'Coppedehalle' was in use at least as early as 1258. There are several reasons suggested for the name. It may derive from the Cobbing Brook that runs by Epping into the River Lea, or it may refer to the towers of the original house which may have been 'coped' or covered with lead. The most likely reason is a reference to the 'cop' or eminence upon which the site stands, perched as it is about 300 feet above sea level above the surrounding valleys. This position is best appreciated when catching sight of the house from the M25 which runs across the park.

This book describes what we know of the houses that were built on the site and the people who lived in them. It tries to put them in their social and historical context: the Forest, the King, the influence of the Church, the Civil War, the rise of the wealthy middle classes, the Industrial Revolution, two world wars and the society which emerged after them. All these influences affected Copped Hall and are very good reasons to preserve it and try to tell its story. No one family dominated this house as great families did in other places, its fortunes waxed and waned with the fortunes of its owners and that is where its fascination and value to the community lie. Copped Hall is a reminder of the whole spectrum of English history.

THE MEDIEVAL HOUSE

THE FORESTERS

Before the Norman Conquest the manor of Eppinga was given to the abbots of Waltham Abbey by King Harold. It was taken away by King William because of their association with Harold and given to William's brother Bishop Odo of Bayeux. He acquired 80,000 acres of land in Essex to create the Great Forest of Essex for hunting and brought the land under King William's strict forest laws. Barbaric punishments were meted out for infringements of the laws and the inhabitants were deprived of their rights to wood and game.

Eventually the land was restored to the Abbeys of Barking and Waltham. By the twelfth century the land where Copped Hall stands was a forest where the king could take 'delight and pleasure' in hunting and the monasteries too were privileged to hunt hares and foxes. Each year they received generous gifts of venison from the royal hunters, supplemented by their sheep farms on the Thames estuary and in the Lea Valley.

The administration of the forest was headed by the Lord Warden, who was appointed by the King. Each forest had its own Lord Warden and in Essex the Montfichet family and the Earls of Oxford held the office for many centuries. The Lord Warden appointed the foresters, woodwards, agisters and reeves, who carried out the day-to-day work in the forest. There were also foresters in fee who were a superior type of forester, appointed by the King. Henry Fitzaucher of Copped Hall was a forester in fee and it was his duty to make "wanlace" (bring the deer to bay) when the King came hunting in the forest.

Parallel to the administration, the forest judiciary was led by the Chief Justice of all the Forests, another royal appointment. Below him were the Verderers who were elected for each forest by the freeholders of the county. They were the equivalent of JPs and presided at two forest courts, the Court of Attachments and the Swainmote, which protected the 'vert and venison' and the exclusive right of the King to hunt deer.

THE FITZAUCHERS

The Fitzaucher family held Copped Hall and enjoyed the privileges and income from their position as forester from about 1150, when they were given the manor of Copped Hall to hold in fee of the Abbey of Waltham and of the King by serjeancy from King Richard. The lands belonged to various members of the family, notably Aucher the younger brother of Orgar who was named in a Royal Charter as serving the king as a huntsman and who also held the manor of High Laver, which possession was to cause so much trouble later on. In 1188 Copped Hall passed to Aucher's son William and by then King Henry II had granted two acres of land to the Hall and its surrounding garden. This site was in the parish of Waltham Holy Cross and the house would have been a large, single-storied timber framed hall with service rooms attached.

The most quarrelsome member of the family was the second Richard who inherited in 1234 on the death of his elder brother. His succession to the manor of High Laver was disputed by the local Abbess and the quarrel was only settled three years later. Richard was killed in another quarrel in 1253, to be succeeded by his son Stephen. The lands at High Laver were still causing trouble, this time with the Abbey of Waltham to which the estate had been transferred. There was an agreement that the Abbot would farm the lands for eight years in lieu of rent from the Fitzauchers but when Stephen died in 1267 at the end of the eight years, Henry his brother refused either to pay rent to the Abbey or to allow them to farm the land. Various bitter accusations and then outright violence followed, in the course of which two Fitzaucher servants were killed and many Abbey servants wounded. The dispute was settled in favour of the Abbey by the Courts in 1275.

By 1303 the park at Copped Hall had grown to 60 acres with arable land of 100 acres and meadow lands of 20 acres, a considerable estate inherited by Henry's son who married an heiress with estates in Skipton in Yorkshire. He continued to live at Copped Hall during Edward 111's reign until 1337 when the estate to Sir John Shardlowe. It was done in such a way that Aucher retained an interest in Copped Hall for the remainder of his lifetime. Sir John, his wife Joan and brother Thomas only kept the estate until 1350 when the manors of Copped Hall and Shingle Hall were sold to the Abbot of Waltham Abbey for the sum of £130 6s. 8d and in exchange for manors at Boreham in Essex and one in Cambridgeshire.

MEDIEVAL MONASTERIES

English monasticism is as old as English Christianity. St Augustine and his followers, who came to Canterbury in AD 547, lived by the Benedictine rule and St Aidan, who evangelized the North of England, lived in a strict Celtic style.

However, the Viking invasion destroyed most of these communities and the oldest monasteries in England were refounded by St Dunstan's followers in the Benedictine tradition. The Cistercians were founded in the twelfth century. They lived mainly in remote valleys where they could find solitude and follow a simple disciplined way of life in elaborate buildings. At this time also the Augustinians arose, dedicated to teaching and evangelism, and establishing small houses near to towns and castles, bringing Christianity to the local people. In the thirteenth century orders of friars were founded. They lived on charity, and were dedicated to teaching and preaching to the people. By 1348 when the Black Death struck Britain there were nearly 1,000 religious houses in England and an estimated 14,000 men and 3,000 women were living the religious life.

The religious orders lived in communities, in obedience to a head, an abbot, abbess, prior or prioress; they took vows of celibacy, wore distinctive dress and lived in poverty, although some of the communities were very rich indeed.

The prime function and first responsibility of all of them was to maintain the daily cycle of prayer. Eight times a day, spread at intervals through the day and night, they would meet to sing or recite the daily offices or celebrate the mass. Many benefactors gave money to the abbeys and monasteries for prayers to be said for them, which made some places very wealthy.

The abbots of the more important houses like Waltham Abbey found themselves obliged to serve the Crown in various capacities as well as sit in the upper house of Parliament. These men often no longer shared the communal life of their abbey but lived in secular style in a separate establishment with their own servants and their recreation was spent in hunting and hawking, like the local gentry.

WALTHAM ABBEY

With the acquisition of the Hall and deer park and the later return of the hereditary office of Verderer which had lapsed at the departure of the Fitzauchers, the Abbots of Waltham Abbey had added considerably to their wealth and they set about enlarging the estate, extending the park by about 120 acres towards Epping in 1374. The Abbot described Copped Hall as 'a mansion of pleasure and privacy' that was exclusively for his own use.

One of their duties was to provide hospitality for kings who came to Waltham seeking pleasure in the form of hunting or spiritual refreshment; for example Henry III was entertained at Copped Hall for spiritual purposes, Richard II sought retreat there at the end of the Peasants Revolt in 1381 and a frequent royal visitor on hunting trips was Henry VIII.

THE DISSOLUTION

The Roman Catholic Church with its monasteries was an extremely powerful influence in medieval England. Waltham Abbey was one of the most powerful. It owned enormous areas of land and held sway over the markets, courts and minds of the men and women who lived as the Abbey's tenants. The Abbot lived the aristocratic life, with secular pastimes such as hunting, and wielded much political power.

However, the Church was becoming more corrupt during the fourteenth and fifteenth centuries. Geoffrey Chaucer showed this in the most famous poem of the period 'The Canterbury Tales'.

This book, still unfinished when the poet died, is Chaucer's best known work. It is the account of a pilgrimage to Canterbury and the stories that the pilgrims tell to while away the time on the journey, competing for a prize for the best story which is offered by the landlord of the inn at Southwark from where they set out. The storytellers span the whole range of society from the knight and his squire down to the humble ploughman. The pilgrims are a mixed group, some righteous and others rascally, especially those from the Church. Chaucer describes the gentle clerk of Oxford, the cultivated and sensitive Prioress and the saintly village parson. There are also such social dregs as the Pardoner, a man licensed to sell papal indulgences and pardons, who carried supposed relics of holy saints like a pillowcase which he said was a piece of St Mary's veil and his companion the Summoner, whose job was to enforce the laws of the ecclesiastical court, who was not above taking bribes.

The worldly monk is described as follows...
> "A monk there was, a fair for the maistrie
> An outrider, that loved venerie,
> A manly man, to be an abbot able.
> Full many a dainty horse had he in stable.....
> Greyhounds he had, as swift as fowl in flight:
> Of pryking and of hunting of the hare
> Was all his lust, for no cost would he spare....
> And for to fasten his hood under his chin
> He had of gold y-wrought a full curious pin,
> A love knot in the greater end there was".

His chief delight was hunting, and he dressed in the most expensive furs and gold ornaments.

There was also a friar who was too friendly with his female penitents and very good at abstracting money from the poor of the parish. The corruption of the Catholic Church which to some extent led to the dissolution of the monasteries is well documented in these characters.

The tide of protest about such corruption was sweeping Europe and Martin Luther was instrumental in bringing about a new movement we call 'Protestantism'. He was born in Saxony in 1483 and became a monk but came to believe that heaven could be attained "by faith alone" and a belief in the mercy of God. He proposed a change in the Christian religion based on the individual's ability to approach God on his own account, not through a priest, and his right to read the Bible in his native tongue. In 1521 at the Diet of Worms he challenged the Catholic Church and new ideas were argued all over Europe.

This new movement only needed a trigger to take hold in England. This occurred when Henry VIII, who had been named 'Defender of the Faith' by the Pope, came up against the power of the Church when he tried to divorce Catherine of Aragon. His desire for a male heir to prevent the wars that had devastated England in the last struggle for the succession during the Wars of the Roses forced him to secede from Rome and declare himself head of the Church in England.

In 1529, when Henry was seeking a means of ending his marriage, an outbreak of plague in Cambridge brought Thomas Cranmer to Waltham to stay with two of his pupils. In conversation with two of Henry's advisers, Cranmer suggested that the king might seek the advice of the universities of Europe as to the legality of his marriage to Catherine over the head of the Pope, and so began the process which led to the Reformation in England and the breaking of the power of the Catholic Church which had had such a stranglehold on the government of the Kingdom.

WALTHAM ABBEY
by James Keith ARPS

Abbot Fuller apparently strove to save Waltham Abbey from the process of Dissolution, which began with small failing abbeys and took on momentum after 1535, by presenting Copped Hall to the King, but it was unavailing and Waltham Abbey was the last monastic house in England to be dissolved. In 1540, Abbot Fuller and the remaining eighteen canons surrendered and together with the servants of the Abbey were pensioned off with very generous lump sums and annual payments, possibly the first redundancy packages! The possessions of the Abbey were sold off or taken by the king and in 1541 Henry leased most of the Abbey lands to Anthony Denny of Cheshunt.

In 1544, plans were made to demolish the Abbey, but the townsfolk protested that their parish church was at the east end of the monastery and so the present building was saved for parish use while the rest of it was reduced to rubble.

HENRY VIII

Henry VIII was a frequent visitor to Waltham Abbey and probably stayed at the monks' forest retreat at Copped Hall. He and his daughter Elizabeth were keen huntsmen, and often hunted in the forests at Hatfield and Waltham. Henry built the standing at Chingford known as "Queen Elizabeth's Hunting Lodge" where the court would gather to watch the chase.

In the grounds of Copped Hall there was an avenue of yew trees, with a statue of Henry at one end and his son Edward VI at the other. The story goes that on the morning of May 19th 1536, Henry paced up and down this walk, waiting for the distant sound of a cannon from the Tower of London to signal that his second wife Anne Boleyn had been executed. As the cannon sounded Henry is said to have mounted his horse and ridden off to Theobald's at Waltham Cross where Jane Seymour waited. The couple were married soon after. A new avenue of yews was planted in the year 1999 in what is believed to be the same position by the Friends of the Copped Hall Trust, who appealed for local donations of £10 per tree and planted 140 seedling yews. They also tested whether a gun could be heard from the place and distinctly heard the sound of a royal salute from the yew tree walk, in spite of the M25 and other modern traffic.

KING HENRY'S WALK IN 1999
by Sylvia Keith ARPS

THE SHORT REIGN OF EDWARD VI

After Henry's death his only son Edward VI came to the throne. He was only nine years old but was an ardent devotee of Protestantism. Under the influence of his advisers the laws of the country were altered so that the old religion was gradually outlawed and it became a criminal offence to say Mass. Mary Tudor, his elder half-sister, was an ardent Catholic, like her mother, Catherine of Aragon, and for a while at least during Edward's short reign stayed at Copped Hall. In 1547 Sir Robert Rochester was managing Mary's finances and was appointed Comptroller of her household. On 22nd of March 1551 he was examined by the Council as to the number of Mary's chaplains, and on August 14th ordered, in spite of his protests, to take measures that no-one should say or hear Mass in her household. He returned to Copped Hall but he could not bring himself to carry out these orders and acknowledged his readiness to go to prison instead. Rochester was sent to the Tower but the next year was released "for the weakness of his body" and allowed to retire to his country house, but he suffered the loss of his title and his lands at Little Laver.

Like her father and brother, Mary was arrogant, proud and strong willed and the principal officer of her household, Sir Edward Waldegrave, was no match for her. She persisted in keeping her chaplains and saying Mass in her private chapel at Copped Hall. Sir Edward was sent to the Tower for his weakness. (Mary released him upon her accession and made him Chancellor of the Duchy of Lancaster and Lieutenant of Waltham Forest. Sadly, the Protestant Queen Elizabeth returned him to the Tower when she became queen and he died there in 1561.)

Later in August 1551 the Privy Council sent for Mary's three officers and commanded them to inform their mistress and her chaplains that there were to be no more Roman Catholic ceremonies at Copped Hall but on their return Mary forbade them from delivering their message. The report says that, "she seemed to be marvellously offended with them". She sent them back with a letter to the King dated from her "poor howse at Copped Hall 19th Auguste 1551", stating her rights and defiance of their orders.

Lord Chancellor Rich, Sir William Petre and Sir Anthony Wingfield were then sent with a letter from the King ordering her to obey the will of the Privy Council. Once again she defied them reminding them of the promise made to the Emperor of Spain that she would be able to continue in her religion, and pointing out to them whose daughter she was, "who made the more parte of you almoste of nothinge". She asked for the return of her Comptroller of the Household because she said she was unused to baking and brewing and organising her own accounts. Sir Robert Rochester was allowed to resume his position in her household.

The Princess then went in person to her brother and pointed out that though her earthly part supported the king, her soul belonged to God and she would not change. The next day the King received a declaration of war from the Emperor's Ambassador if Mary was molested. Archbishop Cranmer advised the King, "to wink at the use of the Mass for a while" and he gave up in disgust and fury. In the first year of her reign Mary took her revenge on Lord Rich by ordering him to be present at the burning of Protestant martyrs in various parts of Essex and to help the sheriff in the executions.

MARY TUDOR

In 1553 Edward died of tuberculosis, and the Protestant lords put Lady Jane Grey on the throne in order to avoid having a Catholic queen. This was a very unpopular move with the people of London who believed strongly in the sanctity of the legal succession and venerated the Tudor dynasty. Mary Tudor went to her estates at Framlingham in Suffolk and then with a force of 2000 men marched on London to claim her throne. Jane was deposed, imprisoned and executed with her husband, having been queen for only nine days. Mary began therefore with a wave of popularity but this was eroded when she insisted on marrying the

Spanish King Philip She was already thirty seven years old and desparately wanted a Catholic heir for England. She returned the country to Catholic practices and reinstated the power of the Pope, another unpopular move. Public burnings of heretics followed. By the time Mary died in 1558, over 300 men and women had burned for their faith, including Thomas Cranmer, who recanted for fear of the stake, but when he realised he was to burn anyway, put his right hand that had signed the recantation into the flames first. Another reason for her unpopularity was a disastrous war with France which cost England its last French possession, the port of Calais.

Rochester's fidelity to the queen was rewarded with many honours: he was made Comptroller of the royal household, created a knight of the Bath at the queen's coronation and made one of the Privy Council. His voice carried a great deal of weight in the council's decisions. He was appointed by Philip of Spain, the queen's husband, to look after his affairs during his absence and entrusted with other important commissions. He died in 1557.

QUEEN ELIZABETH I

Queen Elizabeth came to the throne on a new tide of popular sentiment. She was young, a Tudor and a Protestant. Sir Thomas Cornwallis had leased Copped Hall from the previous monarch for twenty one years and the Queen sent Commissioners to find out…

"what spoil, waste or destruction hath been made to any of our timber trees, woods or underwoods growing and being within the same our said park, and what pales, rails and posts or gates in and about the same hath been lately pulled down, spoiled, defaced or carried away, as also what spoil, hurt, or ruin hath been made or done in and about our said Manor House…."

The reply was that Henry Cornwallis had pulled down two partitions of the Manor House to make a brewing house and had destroyed a door and hinge with its lock in that room. In the park he had cut down seven trees making about fourteen loads of timber worth about ten pounds, which were used to make various pieces of furniture for the mansion, including sixteen bedsteads, as well as tables and a window with shelves. The impression given was that the house was in a sad state of disrepair and that the park had been neglected and exploited for the gain of the occupant. This was not really true, the wood had been used to the benefit of the Hall but as he was technically guilty of "decay" by cutting down the trees the charge served as an excuse to rid Copped Hall of a Catholic tenant in 1563 and clear the way for a new owner.

There is only very sketchy evidence as to what the house was like in medieval times but it seems to have been a hunting lodge with a high end to the west. The three storeys were reached by a spiral staircase, built in brick, with a flat roof from which one could view the hunt, and turrets. It had a fashionably vertical emphasis and bay windows in the main chamber on the first floor, looking out to the courtyard. It seems to have been altered by 1562 with the addition of a moat, new staircases, ogee turrets and viewing platforms on the roof with arcaded shelters to make the viewers of the hunt more comfortable in bad weather, and new windows.

CHAPTER TWO
THE TUDOR MANSION

THE HOUSE THAT HENEAGE BUILT

In 1564 Queen Elizabeth gave Copped Hall to Sir Thomas Heneage. Sir Thomas had married Anne, daughter of Sir Nicholas Poyntz, and their daughter Elizabeth was born in 1556. In July 1568 the Queen visited Copped Hall on a royal progress through Essex. The Queen knighted Sir Thomas at Windsor and appointed him Keeper of the Records at the Tower of London, with his brother. In 1585 he was elected Member of Parliament for Essex, where he served until his death. Also in 1585 he sat with Sir Walter Raleigh on an enquiry into the ransom of English captives in Barbary. He was Treasurer of War during the Armada, responsible for the payment and victualling of the English fleet. It was this post that brought him the Armada Jewel, a rich ornament with the Queen's profile shown on it, a very lavish gift from a rather parsimonious lady! By 1589 he was Vice-Chamberlain of the Royal Household and a Privy Councillor and the next year he was appointed Chancellor of the Duchy of Lancaster and High Steward of Hull. This bare outline of his career indicates the esteem in which the Queen held him and her nickname for him of "Sanguine" bears witness to his level head and intelligence.

By 1568 at the time of the queen's visit, he had incorporated the old hall into a substantial brick built mansion, designed by John Thorpe. This mansion was the grandest of the three houses that have been built at Copped Hall. It consisted of a large south-facing central block, complete with entrance hall. To either side

SIR THOMAS HENEAGE
Courtesy of Lord Petre

were east and west wings. A screen wall was built later to enclose the north side and create an inner courtyard. The east wing contained the service quarters and had substantial cellars underneath running also under some of the central block, the remains of which can still be traced. The largest room in the house was the long gallery, which ran the length of the east wing on the first floor. It was fifty six yards long and was said to be "the most proportionable gallery in England." The west wing was not so large and was barely linked to the main block. Only one column of the main house still remains standing at the site. Formal gardens were laid out to the south of the house, with kitchen gardens to the sides. The house stood at the Waltham end of the garden, facing north towards Waltham, and there were 103 rooms and hallways and 53 hearths, a very large house indeed!

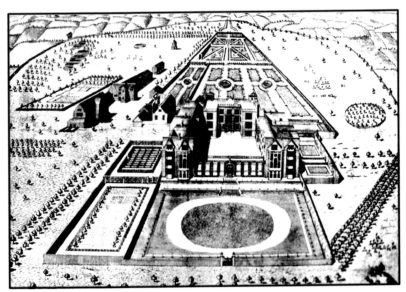

THE HOUSE THAT HENEAGE BUILT
from the Essex Record Office

Sir Thomas's wife Anne died and he married for the second time in 1594. His new wife was Mary, Countess of Southampton. She was the mother of Harry Wriothesley the Earl of Southampton, the patron of the playwright and poet William Shakespeare.

The festivities at that wedding probably included the first performance of the play "A Midsummer Night's Dream", specially written for the occasion by Shakespeare for his patron's mother's wedding party. This was a very suitable piece for the marriage of two older people, dealing as it does with the marriage festivities of a mature Duke, Theseus of Athens, with the Amazon Queen Hippolyta, and the courtship of four young people, while the common folk prepare a play to celebrate the wedding and the fairies squabble over the possession of a changeling child. Stewart Trotter in his interesting book "Love's Labour's Found" proposes that the play took place over several days, beginning and ending in the Long Gallery, but with scenes taking place out of doors around the park, and indeed there are many descriptions of outdoor settings and various times of day to support this theory. The moonlit forest scenes would be played in the forested valleys that surround the mansion, the various trees mentioned, the Duke's oak where the mechanicals meet for their rehearsal and the hawthorn brake which becomes their tiring-house, may have been real trees on the estate and the bank where the wild thyme blows and oxlips and violets bloom, a real bank somewhere in the grounds. Perhaps even, the hounds described in the play.....
"With ears that sweep away the morning dew;
        Crook-kneed and dewlapp'd like Thessalian bulls
        Slow in pursuit, but match'd in mouth like bells,
        Each under each;"
really belonged to Heneage and were heard in the play. At any rate I would like to think it might have been so.

18

Though the marriage was reputedly very happy, it only lasted fifteen months, as Sir Thomas died the following year. He was buried in St. Paul's in 1595 alongside his first wife Anne. The monument to him was badly damaged in the Great Fire of London in 1666, but what remains of it was remounted and can be seen today in the crypt.

Copped Hall was left to his wife Mary and on her death to his daughter Elizabeth and her husband Sir Moyle Finch.

HENEAGE'S DAUGHTER ELIZABETH

When Elizabeth, Lady Moyle Finch, inherited Copped Hall she was heard to say that she would gladly give it to anyone who could persuade the king to raise her to the rank of Countess alongside her stepmother whom she had detested because she was a Countess whilst Elizabeth was a mere baronet's wife. Her remark was overheard by Lionel Cranfield, an ambitious man who owned Pishiobury in Sawbridgworth.

When he became Lord High Treasurer he remembered her words and devised a complex plan to obtain her wish for her, get Copped Hall for himself, and do a favour for one of the King's favourites, the Duke of Richmond and Lennox, who was Lord Steward of the Royal Household and a kinsman of the king. Pishiobury was worth about £10,000, the size of a debt owed by the Duke. James 1 agreed to make Elizabeth Finch a Countess and Cranfield paid off the Duke's debts in return for receiving Copped Hall. Unfortunately King James went back on his word and she became only Viscountess Maidstone, but in 1628 Charles 1 made good his father's promise and she was created Countess of Winchelsea.

The Countess went to live in Winchelsea House on the Epping Road which was then part of the estate and one of the original manor houses in Epping. This house was a three gabled building with tall chimneys and a flight of steps at the front. During the eighteenth and early nineteenth centuries it became a prosperous coaching inn, known as Epping Place Inn. The basement of the house is all that remains of it, underneath the house now known as Epping Place, next door to the house called Winchelsea House on Epping High Road. Countess Winchelsea only lived for another five years to enjoy her title before she died in 1633.

Her eldest son, Sir Heneage Finch, Recorder of London and Speaker of the House of Commons, had died two years before, and his younger brother, when he became Earl of Winchelsea, sold the house to William, Lord Grey of Wark.

LIONEL CRANFIELD

Lionel Cranfield was born in 1575 into a family of merchants. He was a clever man with money but devoid of tact and diplomacy when dealing with people. While he became wealthy, he made many enemies by his harsh and unyielding attitude. He also got involved in the very dangerous political situation of the Stuart period. He endeared himself to King James 1, (who was the son of Mary Queen of Scots, the lady executed by Elizabeth 1, and already James VI of Scotland).

James inherited the financial problems of the Tudors because he too had to pay for his government out of his own purse and could only appeal to Parliament for funds in time of war. James was fond of handsome young men, although he was a middle-aged man with three children, and he showered his favourites with lavish gifts of money, titles and property. His court was extremely corrupt and extravagant. Lionel Cranfield was also the friend of the most notorious and hated of the king's favourites, George Villiers, Duke of Buckingham, younger son of a Leicestershire gentleman and reputed to be the most handsome man of his age. Lionel rather reluctantly married the Duke's mother's cousin, Anne Brett, his second wife.

When Cranfield became Surveyor General of Customs he managed to increase the Crown's income by £30,000 a year within two years, a very useful sum for the King. In 1619 he was given the job of Master of the Court of Wards. This post was considered extremely lucrative for its possessor and led to huge abuses of power and privilege. Cranfield put a stop to the abuses, thus helping still more to restore James's finances. In 1621 he was made Lord High Treasurer and the next year the King created him the Earl of Middlesex. All these upward steps bore witness to his favour with the king, but his methods made him many enemies in the Court and in Parliament. He also had incurred the anger of the Prince of Wales and the Duke of Buckingham by opposing war with Spain. In 1624 Sir Dudley Carlton wrote of him, "The world cries 'Down with him'; there has been no man in England these last two hundred years whose ruin has been so thirsted after by all sorts of people".

His meteoric upward career was brought to an abrupt end when Parliament impeached him, accusing him of all manner of charges, "bribery, extortion, oppression and other grievous misdemeanours". In spite of King James trying to intercede on his behalf for mercy and justice, on the 13th May 1624 the Lords sent for the Commons to come and hear the judgment against the Lord Treasurer.

LIONEL CRANFIELD, FIRST EARL OF MIDDLESEX
by Daniel Mytens (in a private collection)

Cranfield was brought before the full House and bowed and kneeled until told he might stand up. He was found guilty and sentenced to lose all his offices and from then on be ineligible for any Government post, to be imprisoned in the Tower of London during the King's pleasure, to be fined £50,000, and neither sit in Parliament or even come near it for the rest of his life.

Two years later, after a short spell in prison, he retired to Copped Hall, Charles 1, who succeeded to the throne in 1625, having commuted his fine to £5,000, his sugar farm and his house in Chelsea. He was an angry and embittered man, and took no further part in politics. One of the first things he did upon his enforced retirement was engage the services of Edmund Kinsman, mason to Inigo Jones, who had worked on Lionel's house in Chelsea. The loggia was rebuilt with the columns facing the inner courtyard rather that the garden. It had a balustraded parapet on the garden side, the walls "pierced with window-like appendages on either side of the gateway with a scrolled pediment" and he also restored both wings of the house.

In 1631 is recorded in the Parish Register the burial of one of Lionel's sons, called William.

In 1639 Copped Hall was hit by a great hurricane which blew along the gallery forcing the stones of the great east window all the way through the fifty six yard length of it. In Farmer's History of Waltham the event is described in detail; "Here happened a Hurricane, or wild wind, which, entering in at the great east window, blew that down....with the picture of the lord Coventry singled from many more which were hung on both sides, untouched all the length of the gallery....out of the West Window, which it threw down to the ground. It seems the wind, finding this room in the form of a trunk.....forced the stones of the first window like pellets clear through it".

There are extant in the Kent Records Office the accounts of Lionel Cranfield for some days in October of the year 1640, the year following the hurricane. A large number of ridge tiles, ordinary tiles, several hundred nails and 200 feet of board were paid for, which may well have been used to repair or secure the house before the winter.

It is also interesting to note that over 300 pounds of beef and veal were bought as well as 3 bushels of salt (a bushel weighed about 47 lbs.). The farmers would kill off their bulls and male calves as winter approached, so that they would not be put to the expense of feeding them through the winter and all this meat would be salted down to preserve it.

The wage for a labourer in 1640 was 10d a day, the equivalent of 4p in present currency. Also for 10d Lionel bought a quire of gilt paper for his daughter Frances, then about 16 years old, who later married Richard Sackville and thus brought Copped Hall into that family, and a quire of cheaper paper for his younger son, Lionel, aged then 15, for the sum of 5d.

Lionel Cranfield lived at Copped Hall until 1645, tending the property, growing asparagus, cauliflowers, other vegetables, and many kinds of fruit such as gooseberries, cherries and "trees of Kentish pippins". He also cultivated flowers in his gardens, yellow double roses, double violets and, most interesting of all perhaps, he grew yellow tulips at the time that "tulip mania" was sweeping Holland and England, when a tulip bulb might change hands for as much as the price of a house! Possibly he was the first man in Essex to grow tulips.

He gathered many pictures and books at Copped Hall and collected a very fine library, which he shared with his friend Dr. Thomas Fuller, the curate of Waltham. Fuller described the library to Cranfield's son as "the numerous and choice library at Copt Hall," and remarked that judging the Earl by his library, "he may be said to have been his own tutor and his own university".

THE CIVIL WAR, 1642 – 1649

When Charles 1 tried in vain to arrest five members of Parliament, he dismissed all the members and tried to rule without a Parliament but created such ill feeling that he became increasingly unpopular in the country. For the first time England was split into two warring factions, those who supported the King and those who supported Parliament. Charles was forced to make his headquarters at Oxford and his soldiers were under the leadership of his nephew, Prince Rupert. The Parliamentary force, led by Oliver Cromwell and Sir Thomas Fairfax, enjoyed the massive support of London and the south east counties. The first battle was fought at Edghill in 1642 but the outcome was indecisive. On the whole the early years of the war went in the King's favour. Rupert was a fine commander and his lightly armed cavalry attacked the ill-equipped and inexperienced Roundheads (called this for the shape of their helmets). However, in 1644 the Roundheads won a decisive victory at the battle of Marston Moor and the next year Cromwell created his New Model Army, nationally organised and regularly paid, with promotion depending on ability not rank. In June 1645 this army won the battle of Naseby, effectively bringing the Cavalier resistance to an end and King Charles was forced to flee.

He surrendered to the Scots, but they handed him over to his English enemies. He was put on trial on the charge of treason for waging war against his own people. The trial lasted a week and he was found guilty and publicly executed three days later at Whitehall, the only British monarch to meet such a fate.

In the struggle between Parliament and Charles 1 and during the Civil War, Lionel Cranfield maintained a neutral attitude. In 1642 he begged the King to excuse him from service on account of the fact that he was sixty seven years old and so weak that he could not walk without the aid of a staff and was unable to ride three miles on a horse. In 1644 he begged the Parliamentary Commissioners to excuse him from paying exorbitant sums to them to pay for the war on the grounds that he was "an old weak man" and also pleaded that the County of Essex be excused too.

On his death at the age of seventy a magnificent tomb was erected to him in Westminster Abbey with his second wife and this may still be seen near Poets' Corner.

LIONEL CRANFIELD'S SONS

Lionel Cranfield's elder son, James, was as doubtful in his allegiances during the struggles between Parliament and the King as his father. He was born in 1621, when his father was at the height of his wealth and influence. His godparents were the King himself, the Duke of Buckingham, the most powerful man in the realm and the Countess of Lennox, wife of the man for whose benefit Copped Hall was exchanged some years later. He succeeded to the title of Earl of Middlesex at the height of the Civil War and in 1646 Parliament made him Lord Lieutenant of

Staffordshire. However he was imprisoned the following year for "acting against the Army".

In the very next year he was a Commissioner from the Lords to the King but was so shocked by the trial and execution of Charles 1, as were so many of the people of England, that he retired to his estate at Copped Hall and lived there until his death in 1651. He died childless and the estate passed to his brother (another Lionel), who became the third Earl of Middlesex at the age of twenty six.

OLIVER CROMWELL

Cromwell led an unremarkable life until 1642, when he led a cavalry unit in East Anglia. After Charles' execution he tried to rule with Parliament but realised they were as corrupt as the King had been. He dismissed them and had himself proclaimed Lord Protector. He ruled as a dictator but he was a strong and charismatic man able to impose his will on the country.

He was devoutly religious and insisted on the country following a Puritan lifestyle, abolishing Christmas and Mayday celebrations, forbidding drinking and swearing, and requiring everybody to go to church. He became very unpopular with the majority of people, although the well organised armed services brought victory over the Dutch and the Spanish, from whom he captured Jamaica in 1655.

Within two years of his death, after his son Richard had tried to rule, Parliament invited Charles 1's son, Charles 11, to return to rule.

CHARLES 11

This Charles, known as the "merry monarch", was greeted with great enthusiasm by the people. He enjoyed eating and drinking, gambling, hunting and boating. He had 17 mistresses, including Nell Gwynne, by whom he had 2 children, but he had no legitimate heir.

During the Protectorate, when Cromwell dominated the life and politics of England, Lionel Cranfield, the younger son of the first Earl, obtained a licence to travel on the Continent. At first his sympathies were as unclear as those of his father and elder brother but in 1659 he was imprisoned for "delinquency" and it is clear he had come out openly on the side of the Royalists. He was sent as one of the party of gentlemen on the mission to The Hague to invite King Charles 11, the son of the beheaded King Charles, to ascend the throne of England.

After the Restoration in 1660, the King visited Copped Hall on several occasions. One was recorded by Thomas Gower, who wrote on June 30th of that year to his friend...
"The king dined yesterday at Copt Hall, today at Roehampton, returned both days in terrible rain and thunder, so as the fine feathers and gay clothes are come back utterly spoiled, and the brave gallants look like drowned rats or as if they had been rolled in puddles, and the gilded carriages are become like others.....His Majesty and his royal brothers are daily feasted. Yesterday they were usually entertained at supper; but then the Earl of Middlesex feasted them magnificently at his house at Copt Hall, after they had spent the morning in hunting with great content in Waltham Forest.

P.S. The king went yesterday to Copt Hall to hunt the buck; the lords invite the king very oft, and the two Dukes, and he is very freely merry with them, and he will not have them provide above ten or twelve dishes for him at most". At least the weather has not changed between then and now!

Lionel, the third Earl, was one of the friends of his father's friend, Dr. Thomas Fuller, who was his pastor as curate of Waltham, and presented him as a "library –less Scholar" with his father's much admired collection of books.

He died in 1674 and the estate passed to his nephew, Charles Sackville, Earl of Dorset, as he like his brother had no children. The title then lapsed until it was revived the following year when Charles Sackville was created first Earl of Middlesex.

CHARLES SACKVILLE, 6th EARL OF DORSET

Charles Sackville was the son of the first Earl's youngest daughter Frances, who married Lord Buckhurst who later became the fifth Earl of Dorset. He was something of a tearaway when he was young. When he was about 30 years old, after the Restoration, Samuel Pepys, the famous diarist of the times, describes him as "running up and down all the night, almost naked through the streets, and at last fighting and being beat by the watch" and in 1667 Pepys lamented that Sackville had lured Nell Gwynne away from the theatre and that with another disreputable friend kept "merry house" at Epsom. In the following year the king began his courtship of her.

In 1662 Sackville was indicted with his brother and three others for the robbery and murder of a tanner called Hoppy. The defence was that they were returning one night in February from Waltham to London when he and his friends came upon a group who complained that they had been set upon by violent thieves. They pursued the robbers and caught up with them, but when they were challenged the miscreants fled. In the course of the pursuit Hoppy was fatally wounded as they had mistaken him for one of the highwaymen. They were all arrested and Sackville and his friends had to petition the courts for bail. Sackville's friends were tried for manslaughter, but they were speedily pardoned and set free.

He became the Member of Parliament for East Grinstead and soon became a favourite of King Charles 11. In 1665 he accompanied the Duke of York in the Dutch War and was at the battle of June 3rd when 18 Dutch ships were captured and 14 others destroyed. On the night before the battle he wrote a song, "To all you ladies now at Land"! He was one of the best of the Restoration poets, and Dryden summed up the two sides of his nature when he wrote of Dorset.....

" I will not rake the dunghill of thy crimes,
   For who would read thy life that read thy rhymes"

Charles Sackville was renowned for his hospitality as well as his wit and after he inherited the estate in 1674 he often entertained both King Charles 11 and his brother King James 11 at Copped Hall, indeed King James felt so at home there he felt he could drop in without much prior warning. Once King James had been hunting in Hatfield Forest and decided to stop for dinner at Copped Hall on the way home to London. A messenger was despatched, only to find the Earl away from home and his wife and daughter about to set out for dinner. The butler and the cook had been given time off to visit Waltham Fair and the keys were with them. "So seeing that there was no help for it....by breaking open locks and doors, and with the help of maids, by the time the king had arrived and had both washed and viewed the house and gardens, a very handsome collation was got ready". When the

King went on his way, he met the Earl coming home, who apologised profusely for things being unprepared, but he received the gracious reply, "Make no excuses, it was exceedingly well, and very handsome".

John Churchill, the Duke of Marlborough, was an aide to James 11 and his wife Sarah was a friend and confidante of the young Princess Anne, the younger sister of Mary, wife to the Prince of Orange. When James 11 who was a Catholic attempted to return England to the domination of the Pope however, John Churchill gave his support to the faction who wished to invite William of Orange to rule England as a Protestant monarch. While the issue stood in the balance, Princess Anne took fright and appealed for help to Charles Sackville to help her escape from London. She fled with her friend Sarah and one maid. Charles gave her refuge at Copped Hall on her way north. Macaulay wrote, "On the following morning she set out to Epping Forest. In that wild tract Dorset possessed a venerable mansion, the favourite resort of wits and poets". As she stepped out of the coach her slipper was stuck in the clay and Sackville gallantly drew off his white glove and put it on her foot before resuming the journey. Her fears proved to be groundless, as James was forced to abdicate and flee the country and the Protestant William of Orange became William 111. She returned to London and in her turn succeeded to the throne as Queen Anne.

An extraordinary inventory was drawn up in 1679, of everything in all the rooms of the Copped Hall Tudor Mansion. A summary of this reveals an enormous household consisting of 103 rooms, 3 of which were great dining rooms, and 5 drawing rooms.

The amount of furniture is staggering; in the house were listed at least 250 chairs with backs, some very grand sounding indeed, with 4 upholstered in cloth of silver wrought with silk in one of

CHARLES SACKVILLE, 6TH EARL OF DORSET
by Sir Godfrey Kneller (in a private collection)

the drawing rooms and 18 backed chairs of grey cloth, laced with red and silver lace and cased with red bags, in the great dining room; about 150 stools and small chairs; 69 tables, some of which had table carpets, like the ones in the great dining room where there were 2 Spanish tables with turkey carpets to them; and 170 tapestries, many in sets of 5 or 6 in a room, such as those 5 fine Morlock tapestry hangings which were in the great drawing room with blue walls which led to the gallery.

Among the 50 bedsteads in the house, in my lord's chamber were listed a French bedstead with a mattress, a feather bed and bolster, a Holland quilt, a pillow, 3 blankets, a tester and head cloth, a quilted back and a great quilt, 4 gold curtains, 4 other curtains, a large wooden screen, a looking glass, a walnut knee-table, a pair of stands from London and 19 cane chairs. There was not such luxury of course in the servants' quarters; the husbandman's chamber in the stables had a half-headed bedstead and mattress, a feather bed, a bolster, 2 old blankets and 1 old rug, 1 table, 1 old chest, a pair of old tongs, 1 old chair, a shelf and 2 forms.

The Great Hall contained 4 tables, 7 forms, 10 racks holding 17 muskets, 14 halberds, 16 bucks' heads, 2 maps, a large pair of andirons, a glass lantern and a great bible and stand.

Charles Sackville was a great friend of King William 111, and once the king took refuge at Copped Hall when an attempt was made to kidnap him as he travelled through the forest. From 1689 to 1697 Sackville was Lord Chamberlain of the Household to William 111 and acquired fabulous furniture from the Royal Household as part of his perquisites. These "perks" were the right to the entire contents of the royal apartments after the death of the sovereign and to remove for his private use any items thought to be worn or outdated. Some of these at Copped Hall were five x-framed ceremonial chairs, a silver and damask chair from

Hampton Court stamped 1661, a chair of state upholstered in purple velvet and embroidered with silver thread, complete with its flanking high stools and footstool, dating from 1620-30, magnificent chased brass lock plates on doors bearing the monogram of William 111 and much more furniture and tapestries.

Charles was so extravagant however that he was forced to sell Copped Hall for £20,000 to Sir Thomas Webster and return to his house at Knole near Sevenoaks in Kent, which he inherited from his mother. He took with him to Knole the furniture he owned, portraits of the Cranfield family and a cartouche of the arms of Lionel Cranfield which was mounted on the roof of the Great Hall at Knole. Much of this treasure can still be seen there.

As he grew older his excesses ceased and after the accession of William of Orange he became a Privy Counsellor, Lord Chamberlain and Knight of the Garter. When William was out of the country in the 1690's he was one of the Lord Chief Justices of the Realm. He also was a generous patron of other men of letters, giving a pension to Dryden when he lost the laureateship and recognising the talents of other men of letters.

Alexander Pope, one of the best known of the eighteenth century poets, pronounced his judgment of Charles Sackville's abilities in lines in the church of Withyam in Sussex……
> "Dorset, the grace of courts, the Muses pride
> Patron of arts and judge of nature died.
> The scourge of pride, though sanctified or great,
> Of fops in learning, and of knaves in state;
> Yet soft in nature, though severe his lay,
> His anger moral, and his wisdom gay………"

SIR THOMAS WEBSTER

Sir Thomas came from Nelmes in Hornchurch and was Member of Parliament for Colchester. He was married to Jane Cheek in 1701, the same year that he bought Copped Hall, and they had several children. He was elected Verderer of the Forest of Waltham in 1717.

Sir Thomas is mentioned in Daniel Defoe's "Tour through the Eastern Counties of England, 1722". The rise of an affluent and upwardly mobile class of professional and trades people noted here is very obvious in the owners of the mansion from this time onward….

"It is observable, that in this part of the country there are several very considerable estates, purchased and now enjoyed by citizens of London, merchants and tradesmen such as ….Sir Thomas Webster at Copthall, near Waltham; and several others".

He purchased several other properties including Battle Abbey, which he bought in 1719 from Lord Montagu and the ancient Abbey of Robertsbridge which he bought from the Earl of Leicester. Battle Abbey became more important to Sir Thomas and he spent more time away from Copped Hall. The Abbey became his family seat which his descendants maintained almost continuously until 1976. He neglected Copped Hall, letting it become very run down, and the house was conveyed to Edward Conyers in 1739 in exchange for an estate in Sussex, not far from Battle Abbey. In the same year his son Whistler died at the age of 36. Webster himself lived until 1751.

EDWARD CONYERS

Edward Conyers came from an old Walthamstow family. His father John was a barrister in the Middle Temple, but traced his family back to Hordon, the ancient seat of Sir Christopher Conyers' family and Conyers' seats at Layton, Sockburn and Bishopston in County Durham. He was married to the Hon. Matilda Fermor, daughter of William, Lord Lempster in 1716.

Edward was keen on owning property; he bought extensively in Walthamstow and further afield and in 1734 bought the "capital messuage called Epping Place", built on the foundations of the ruined Winchelsea House, once owned by Sir Thomas Heneage's daughter and moved there with his wife. Eleven years later, having sold the property his wife brought with her, he bought the Manor of Epping, and with it the title of Lord of the Manor, the right to graze animals in the Forest and the right to elect Verderers. By this time the manor of Epping included.....

"Manors of Epping and Copped Hall, Copped Hall Park, capital messuage Epping Place alias Epping Bury, advowson and great tithes of Epping, woodlands called Wintry Woods and Orange Grove, the manor and farm of Campions, 20 messuages, 20 cottages, 30 stables, 1 shop, 1 windmill, 20 barns, 20 gardens, 20 orchards, 800 acres of land, 650 acres of meadow, 1300 acres of pasture, 500 acres of woodland, 600 acres of furze and heath, 25 acres of moorland, 25 acres of marsh, 20 acres of land covered in water, £311 in annual rents in Epping, Waltham Holy Cross, Nazeing, North Weald Basset, Walthamstow, Leyton, and Chingford, 2 closes called Price Fields and properties in Epping."

Having bought Copped Hall, he began to restore the old building, whilst continuing to live at Epping Place, but he died in 1742 and the property passed to his son John.

JOHN CONYERS

John Conyers was then twenty five years old and a graduate of University College, Oxford. He was MP for Reading and then for Essex from 1772 until the year of his death, but he was never known to speak in the House of Commons. In March 1772 Conyers is listed as "pro, present" at the vote on the Royal Marriage Bill, and the following year he voted with the Government over a motion concerning the Middlesex election. These are the only times his presence was recorded. He made the Grand Tour which included visiting Siena, Florence and Venice where he dined on several occasions with his aunt. He was married to Hannah, his first wife who died in 1743, and two years later he married Henrietta Fermour, the third daughter of Thomas, Earl of Pomfret. They had thirteen children, eight of whom survived infancy.

At first he seemed to have no plans to demolish the Tudor house as he had two pictures of the house painted by George Lambert in 1746 with figures in the foreground inserted by Francis Hayman, and a portrait of himself by Francis Hayman posing in front of one of the pictures. The pictures by Lambert were purchased by the Tate Gallery in 1999 for the sum of £300,000, to enlarge their collection of paintings of the great era of English country houses.

His brother in law, Sir Roger Newdigate, was married to Conyers' sister, Sophia. Sir Roger was a gifted amateur architect as well as being MP for Oxford, and he made drawings of the house, the exterior and several features of the interior, including the Great Hall and two of the fireplaces.

JOHN CONYERS AND THE PICTURE OF HIS HOUSE
by Francis Hayman (courtesy of English Heritage)

However, by 1751 plans had been drawn up by John Sanderson for a new Copped Hall at the Epping end of the garden and the Tudor mansion had been demolished. Today, a single pillar marks the site of the old house and the cellars under the north end can still be made out. The younger Conyers obviously preferred the idea of a smaller, more fashionable house in the classical Georgian manner, and in 1748 plans were made for brick earth from Ware, though a local story states that the bricks for Copped Hall were made in moulds invented by the Reverend Edmund Cartwright from clay out of "pisslepot ponds in the forest". In 1751 kilns were built in the park ready for the production of the bricks, the building plans were approved and work began on the new Copped Hall.

CHAPTER THREE
THE GEORGIAN HOUSE

THE NEW COPPED HALL

The house was to be built on a new site south-east of the original house. This meant that the new house was in the parish of Epping, not in Waltham as before, much to the consternation of the parish of Waltham, for the rates of such a large estate were considerable. In 1758, John Conyers was the subject of a lawsuit by Waltham Abbey and the Wake family. In Wake v. Conyers, an action was taken to determine the boundary between Epping and Waltham Holy Cross and three years later another action was brought by Waltham to try to keep the rates from Copped Hall but as the house undoubtedly lay outside its boundaries they had little hope of winning either action, and thus the age-old link with Waltham Abbey was severed.

A valuation of the old Copped Hall in 1742 valued the materials that could be re-used at £1404 15s 6d and estimated the final cost of the new building at £4465 6s 8d. The old bricks were utilised among the new ones as far as they would go. The common red bricks made in the park cost 12s 6d per thousand, but the light coloured bricks for the outside cost £2 10s 0d per thousand!

The house was designed in the austere classical manner of Georgian domestic architecture, with seven windows placed symmetrically on each floor of the east and west fronts and four windows on each storey on the other sides. It had three storeys above ground and a basement. All round the basement was constructed a tunnel faced in brick that kept the damp of the ground from the cellars, with gratings placed at intervals in the roof. In the cellars the principal room was the kitchen, a large stone-flagged room which was two storeys tall with windows on the ground floor level. The most important storey was the first floor with tall windows for the main reception rooms which comprised of the reception hall, the dining room, the drawing room and the saloon which was the largest room of all, designed for parties and dances. On this floor were also placed three large bedrooms for the owner, his wife and the principal guest. The rooms were arranged around a central double stairwell and were built 'enfilade', with one room leading into the next. The ground floor housed the entrance hall, and other living accommodation including rooms for the housekeeper, the butler and the servants' hall, as well as John's office and the Common Parlour where the family ate on informal occasions. On the top floor with its smaller square windows were the bedrooms for the children and the remainder of the household. The facades were unornamented and the chimneys and roof plain.

In 1759, even before the house was finished, while the saloon and staircase were still incomplete, the family moved in. They had been living still at Epping Place while the demolition and building work was going on, but afterwards, Epping Place was leased to William Stokes for an initial 14 year period at an annual rent of £14. Stokes and his descendants established it as an inn, known as Epping Place Inn or New Inn for the next 86 years.

The new mansion was described as…
"a large and nearly square building of white bricks much admired for the closeness and neatness of their jointings, and the symmetry of their forms, having been cast on purpose in moulds of iron; and since its erection this edifice has received very important improvements under the direction of James Wyatt".

THE GEORGIAN MANSION OF COPPED HALL

Adjoining the original mansion at Copped Hall was a very ancient chapel believed to have been used by the Abbots of Waltham when they stayed at the house. It was into this chapel that John Conyers proposed to place the stained glass window, reputed to have been ordered by Ferdinand and Isabella, the monarchs of Spain, to commemorate the marriage of Henry VII's son Arthur to Catherine of Aragon, and intended to be placed in a chapel of Westminster Abbey. As this son died, the window was sent by Abbot Fuller at Waltham Abbey to his private chapel at New Hall, Boreham. Subsequently it was bought by John Conyers, having been buried during the Cromwellian period to protect it from the Puritans, but it was subsequently sold by his son to St. Margaret's Church, Westminster, for £400. That is where the window can still be seen.

John Conyers continued to improve the house during his lifetime. In 1763 he commissioned interior designs from Robert Adam. He was made a Verderer in 1743 and he loved trees. The fine cedars of Lebanon in the garden were said to have been planted by him in 1747 but they were cut down in the twentieth century as they were diseased.

In 1775 Copped Hall was robbed. The full account appears thus in the Annual Register for that year…
"About two in the morning some villains broke into the parlour at Copped Hall, the residence of John Conyers Esq. member for the County of Essex. From the parlour they forced their way into the butler's pantry, where the butler lay in bed. The noise of their entry waking him, one of the ruffians threw the bedclothes over his head, and with both his hands held a cutlass right across his throat swearing that he would kill him if he offered to move or to alarm the family. In this condition he continued for a considerable time, during which he heard the clock strike three, and likewise heard the thieves put the plate into sacks.

As soon as they had finished they all quitted his room except the fellow placed as a guard over him who stayed a few seconds after his accomplices, and then left him threatening that he would blow his brains out if he either rose or called for an hour to come. After remaining quiet near fifteen minutes that butler got up. Finding that his door was locked on the outside, he got through the window and alarmed the family. A number of the servants went immediately in pursuit of the robbers but in vain. It was soon discovered that a four wheeled carriage had stopped and turned round at the park gate.

Two messengers were sent to Bow Street, and two to Curtain Road, with all the particulars of the robbery. In the afternoon Sir John Fielding informed the magistrate of Stratford that a hackney coach number 44 was seen to pass that road in the way from the forest to London early in the morning. The blinds were drawn up and a second person sat on the box. The driver was brought to account about the matter when at length he acknowledged that he drove one Lambert Reading, and five others to Copped Hall in the night between Sunday and Monday, and that on his return, he carried them to a house in Brick Lane Old Street where they deposited the plate. A proper force was immediately sent to the house where they found Lambert Reading in bed with ten loaded pistols at his side with the greatest part of Mr. Conyers' plate. He was taken and examined at Bow Street on Wednesday, and committed to the New Prison, Clerkenwell whence he was removed on Thursday morning to Chelmsford where he took his trial, and was convicted the same day.

After the trial the judge told him to prepare for his approaching fate for that he was to be taken back to prison, and executed on Saturday, before two o'clock; and was executed accordingly". They certainly believed in swift and summary justice in those days!

John had been appointed as a governor of the Foundling Hospital in 1742 and had made a donation of £1,000. Henrietta became involved with the placing of babies from the Foundling Hospital into suitable families in the vicinity of Copped Hall. These orphans would be cared for by their foster families until they were old enough to be returned to the Foundling Hospital to be taught to read and write and be prepared for employment.
He also built cottages on his estate to help tame the "outcasts" of Epping Forest, as did his neighbour, William Palmer of Nazeing.

John and Henrietta had thirteen children, eight of whom survived infancy. Of their children we know that their eldest daughter, Matilda, became an accomplished botanical painter and a book of her work, containing 62 perfectly preserved water-colours on vellum of flowers and plants, many of which would have been grown at Copped Hall, was found by an art dealer who separated the pages and framed them. After some sales in America he offered the Trustees the chance to hold an exhibition and sale at Copped Hall, which was opened in 2004 by Prince Charles. Several pictures were sold there and later, in 2007, the ten pictures remaining were bought by the Trust as part of their acquisitions. Matilda died in 1803 aged fifty and was buried at All Saints, Epping Upland. The second son, Edward, obtained his degree of BA from all Souls College, Oxford in 1775 and an MA in 1779 in preparation for becoming the vicar at All Saints, Epping Upland and then vicar of St. Mary's Church in Walthamstow. He held that living from 1779 until his death in 1822. He enlarged the vicarage beside All Saints into a substantial house and gave land for 6 almshouses on the west side of the churchyard in Walthamstow in 1795. The oldest of John and Henrietta's children, also called John, attended Oxford University and then made the Grand Tour as his father had done. He married in 1773 and inherited Copped Hall on the death of his father in 1775.

THE SECOND JOHN CONYERS

This John Conyers was born in 1748. As soon as he inherited Copped Hall he began a redecoration of the property and employed the architect and designer, James Wyatt. The two lodges at the gates are thought to be his work.

During his life occurred both the French Revolution and the Napoleonic Wars. As the local J.P. he was responsible for organising the local transport for the troops, (he was required by the Paymaster of the 5th Foot Regiment to provide a certain number of carriages and horses to assemble in Epping to take the regiment from Epping to Stratford) but his main interests were not warlike. He was more interested in agriculture and stock breeding, introducing to his farms new strains of cattle from North Devon. The 1807 Survey of Essex shows that his thirty cows produced on an average £13.14s per cow per annum; ten cows giving 5 dozen pounds of butter per week in summer and 2 dozen in winter. An estate map of 1803 shows that the estate comprised of 2,981 acres; 30% arable land, 30% meadowland, about 22% pasture and the rest woodland and buildings. There were nine different farms, the largest of which was Lower Bury Farm at 550 acres. In addition, the estate owned 532 acres of unenclosed forest land.

His other main preoccupation was hunting. He was host to Lord Palmerston on several occasions but Palmerston was wary of the steel traps that Conyers' sons put down around the estate; in about 1806 Palmerston wrote, "I was unpleasantly disturbed by the wire of a spring gun; luckily it was not loaded. Old Conyers says he is sure some dreadful accident will happen some day with them, but he is overruled by the youthful ardour of his sons. In the moonshine he dares not go into any of his woods, and though fond of planting, is afraid of putting his foot into any of his numerous plantations, lest he should leave it behind him".

It was about this time that there was a fashionable cult of country life and country sports, especially fox hunting and shooting. Owners of large estates employed game-keepers to preserve their birds and felt the need to enclose their fields and woods both so that the new ideas of landscaping could be carried out and to give their horses fences to jump over in the chase.

In the 1740's William Kent designed parklands with leafy glades and long vistas with glimpses of classical temples and curving lines. It was at this time that the ha-ha became the fashion, so that one's garden was protected from the cattle in the park, but one's view was not obscured by a wall around the pleasure garden. Later Capability Brown designed great lakes with gently curved edges and lawns with clumps of specimen trees. He made the house the focal point in the landscape, with a long curving drive so that one came upon the splendid view of the house, in its rural setting, around a bend in the road, and this arrangement can still be appreciated as one approaches Copped Hall today.

THE MANSION FROM THE SOUTH

In 1773 John Conyers married Julia Catherine Matthew, the daughter and heiress of William Matthew, who owned slave plantations in Antigua and St. Kitts.

The ships were from Bristol, Liverpool and Glasgow and nobody spoke out against the trade because it was so lucrative; £2,000 bought a sugar plantation in Barbadosand that was the income from it every year thereafter! When John Conyers married, the inventory of the plantation his wife owned included "a pair of old marking irons and a silver brand mark XXX", a list of the negroes, stock, plantation utensils and stores. Against the names of several of these hapless souls was written a brief description such as "notorious runaway" and their age and value. Letters refer to the invasion of the area by the French, (after which many of the slaves seized their opportunitry and absconded), the threatened tax on absentee landlords like Conyers and problems with runaway slaves. A hurricane destroyed the Drews Hill plantation on Antigua in 1783 leaving... "a ruinous dwelling house, fifty one negroes, one half of no value..." and Conyers wrote to his manager to have the slaves moved to his other estate at St. Kitts.

The slave trade was abolished in the Act of 1807 but slavery itself persisted until the colonies were forced to outlaw it in 1833 after immense pressure by William Wilberforce and his colleagues, the slave states in the West Indies receiving £20,000,000 in compensation.

John Conyers and his wife finally separated in 1812 and she received £31,000 per year as maintenance, with £31,000 down to pay her debts and furnish her home. He died in 1813 and left Copped Hall to his eldest son, Henry John Conyers.

HENRY JOHN CONYERS

Henry John Conyers was born in 1782 and was therefore thirty-one when he became owner of Copped Hall and Lord of the Manor. He was also made Deputy Lieutenant of Essex and a Verderer of the Forest.

In politics Henry John was a reactionary and his chief pastime, which dominated his life and thoughts, was hunting. When he was seeking election to his parliamentary seat, his speeches were punctuated with the cry "Tally Ho!" He was rumoured to have spent more than £100,000 on his hunting activities and many stories were told about his exploits on the hunting field. R.F.Bell wrote that "his treatment of foxes on his own property, where the Duke of Richmond used to shoot with him, was as indefensible as his language on the hunting field". Naturally with all this time and money spent on hunting, Copped Hall was neglected and became very shabby and run down during his time there.

In 1834, Thomas Wright, in "The Picturesque Beauties of Britain" described Copped Hall as....

"This stately and elegant mansion, nearly in the centre of a large park, is a conspicuous object on grounds of considerable elevation.....The park, with some other lands included in the estate, forms an enclosure of four thousand acres, of which above four hundred were some time ago an unprofitable waste, covered with hornbeams, pollards and brushwood and infested with lawless bands of wood and deer stealers, whose forefathers, haunting the close covers of Epping Forest, had subsisted by plunder for centuries. By the praiseworthy exertions of the ancestor of the present owner of Copped Hall, a considerable number of these outcasts were reformed, and prevailed upon to live in small cottages built on purpose for them.....He also provided them with labour, and agreed to supply them with firewood…..”

Wright also gives us a story about how the Warren came to be planted….

“An important improvement was also effected in the cultivation of a piece of ground called the Warren, which consists of one hundred and one acres, and was about seventy years ago, offered to a speculating farmer on a lease of forty years, at two shillings and sixpence an acre. He, however, refused these terms, supposing the land absolutely unproductive. The ground was then ploughed and sown with seeds of almost every kind of tree, thrown in indiscriminately, and left to the operations of Nature. The young plants sprang up, and without further attention have thriven with so much vigour as to form one of the finest and most valuable woods in this part of the country”.

In 1843, the following remarks about Copped Hall and its owner were made….

“Copt Hall is remarkably good for the smooth and nicely jointed brickwork of the exterior and the brusque manner of its owner, but he is the spirit of the chase, and Nimrod's hounds apologise for Nimrod's manner”. After paying a tribute to Mr. Conyers as a master and landlord he continues… “The mansion looks cold and solitary at a distance, perched upon a knoll unbroken by intervening foliage; but a spirit of improvement prevails over the asperities of Nature, and the neighbouring forest is a theatre of endless amusement and delightful recreation”.

It is however said that he deliberately cheated his tenants out of their Lopping Rights, the right of forest residents to cut firewood in the Forest. He offered to have his men cut wood for them for several years, and when he stopped doing so, the rights of the tenants had lapsed because they had not exercised them for a number of years. He had the reputation, not surprisingly, of being a selfish landlord.

At this time the struggles concerning the Enclosure Acts and the right of landlords and others to fence off parts of the Forest were beginning to be questioned, and Henry John was in the forefront of those who wished to put up fences through the forest. The Conyers family as Lords of the Manor were naturally in favour of enclosure, especially as they owned a large tract of Epping Forest.

In 1848 a Committee of the House of Commons agreed to the enclosure of Hainault Forest and the disaforestation of Epping Forest with however a proviso that a portion should be retained for the public enjoyment. As a result Hainault Forest was enclosed and the trees grubbed out. The Commissioners for Woods and Forests offered to sell to the Lords of the Manor the forestal rights of the Crown over the waste lands of Epping Forest for about £5.00 an acre. Finally the local people woke up to the danger that they might lose the forest. Protests over the enclosures began to be heard and the rights of the Commoners to be asserted. The largest enclosure, about 1300 acres, was that of the Manor of Loughton in the ownership of Mr. Maitland, the vicar of the parish. A fence was erected round his holding and clearing began. A labouring man, Thomas Willingale, led the protests and went to prison along with his sons for his opposition. One son died as a result of his incarceration and much sympathy for the old man was aroused. Finally the Corporation of London intervened on behalf of the Commoners and at a meeting in 1870 the Commons Society decided by only one vote to oppose the enclosure of the Forest. In 1878, many years later and after much argument, the rights in the forest land was bought for £20 an acre from the Lords of the Manor. Finally Queen Victoria in person at a public meeting in 1882 declared that the forest was open to the public and could not ever be enclosed

Henry John died in 1853, leaving three daughters, Julia, Charlotte and Henrietta. None of the three had any children and so the family name died out. The eldest, Julia, married the Hon. Anthony John Ashley, a Barrister, and she lived at Copped Hall until two years after her husband's death. In the census of 1861 they were at home and living in the house were listed the Ashleys, their footman, the cook, two housemaids, a kitchen maid, an errand boy, the gardener with his wife and three children and the groom and his wife.

The Hon. Julia Ashley sold Copped Hall to George Wythes, at which time the estate extended over 4,113 acres.

GEORGE WYTHES

The new owner of Copped Hall was another self made man, George Wythes, the son of a farmer, Thomas Wythes. He was born in Worcestershire in 1811 and left home at an early age. He began by building canals but very soon realised that rail transport was the coming thing.

The Industrial Revolution which led to the growth of factories and towns could not have taken place without the development of a good transport system. Raw materials and finished goods needed to be moved quickly and cheaply, the growing towns needed supplies of food and people needed a safe, comfortable travel system. The roads could not cope with the needs of industry for heavy freight and so, by the end of the eighteenth century, a system of canals carried bulky goods like coal, iron ore and cotton. These canals were expensive to build and maintain, vulnerable to the weather and very slow and unreliable.

Engineers such as Richard Trevithick, Richard Blenkinsop and George Stephenson were developing steam engines at the beginning of the nineteenth century, firstly conceived to carry coal from the mines; then in 1825 the first public railway in the world partly powered by locomotive was opened between Stockton and Darlington.

In 1824, a proposal was made for a Liverpool and Manchester Railway and George Stephenson was engaged for the project. Against strong opposition from landowners, conservationists and sceptics the line was built and opened in 1830. The "Rocket" took six and a half hours to travel the 70 miles, getting up to a speed at times of 20 mph.

From 1835 a railway mania gripped the nation and vast fortunes were made (and lost) by people who were tempted to speculate in railway stocks and shares. Many more lines were built, notably the Great Western Railway from London to Bristol designed by Isambard Kingdom Brunel. By 1851, 6,877 miles of track joined all the main centres of population; they carried 80,000,000 passengers a year and employed 130,000 men.

George Wythes went to work on the building of the new railways, on Eastern Counties and South Western Railways and the Brighton line. He also worked in France, Holland, Canada, South America, Spain and the U.S.A. but his big chance came when he was a foreman platelayer and went with his friend Mr. Treadwell to India. Treadwell, who had the contract to build railways there, died on the voyage and George seized the opportunity to take over and made a great success of the venture, returning home with much wealth and reputation. He became one of the outstanding contractors of the railway age, personally supervising all the works and shrewdly assessing the developing situation of the rise of the industrial revolution of the nineteenth century.

He was a private individual by nature and did not become a public figure. Instead, on his retirement in 1861, he bought estates in Surrey, Suffolk, Kent and Essex, the largest being Copped Hall. He devoted his leisure time to farming which he undertook with his usual enterprise and shrewd sense. On his estate at Bickley Park in Kent (which was in the area where his colleague Mr Treadwell had lived) he had a number of roads built and sold off land for the building of many large houses. He also built St. George's Church there for a cost of £12,000. The house eventually became a school. He married Frances Wagstaff and they had one son born in 1839.

His only son, George Edward Wythes, lived at Copped Hall with his wife and two sons until his early death from a diffusive carbuncle in 1875. He was a director of the London, Brighton and South Coast Railway, which his father had had some hand in constructing, a Verderer of the Forest and a J.P. He married twice, firstly Catherine Sarah Jemmett by whom he had two sons, and after her death in 1866, he married Rachel Henty from Nazeing, who gave birth after her husband's death to a daughter, Alice Frances Theodora. The census returns of 1861 record the presence in the house of George himself, aged 32, described as a civil engineer, his wife Catherine, then aged 25, their two small sons aged 3 and 2 respectively, and nine servants. All these servants were born some long way from Copped Hall, in particular the two nurses came from Dorchester and Halifax. The other servants were local and lived on or around the estate. At Little Copped Hall lived the Bailiff, his wife, his mother and his nephew, the gamekeeper and his wife and three children and the coachmen and his wife and baby, quite a house full!

When he died, George Wythes left the house at Bickley to his elder grandson, George Edward Wythes and Copped Hall to the younger grandson, Ernest James. He left an estate reputed to amount to in excess of £2,000,000 divided between his wife and grandchildren.

There was a story among the servants, retold by Clement Harmer, the grandson of the housekeeper in 1879, that a maid, carrying the infant George, accidentally dropped him and caused an injury that stayed with him the rest of his short life. The accident was hushed up and concealed from his parents in case the maid lost her job. This crippled elder son only lived until he was nineteen and thus the whole estate devolved upon the younger son, Ernest James Wythes.

ERNEST JAMES WYTHES

This man, the last resident of Copped Hall, was born in 1868, a year before his grandfather bought Copped Hall. He inherited the whole of the estates on the death of his elder brother in 1887, married Aline Thorold, the eldest daughter of Sir John Henry Thorold, 12th Baronet of Marston, Lincolnshire, in 1894 and set about enlarging and ornamenting the house and garden at Copped Hall.

He employed the architect C.E. Kempe to design two new wings to the house. The one on the north side contained domestic accommodation and bedrooms, and on the south, balancing it, he built an enclosed garden and a covered way which led from the house to a large and elaborate conservatory with a solid back wall and the rest made of wrought iron and glass, containing a round pond and many exotic plants and ferns. He added to the rather plain exterior of the house a terrace outside the first floor on the west side from which access to the garden was gained by two sweeping sets of stone steps. He built a balustrade around the roof and an elaborate triangular pediment above the central façade with sculpted figures and a sundial. Apparently he spent £17,000 on these alterations, a colossal sum in those days.

He kept a very large establishment at Copped Hall. On the night of the census in 1901 he was there with his wife and three small daughters, his father-in-law, his uncle-in-law and twenty seven servants, seven men and twenty unmarried women. Chief among the men was the cook from France, and of the women, five were housemaids, four were laundry maids and there was a nurse and two nursemaids for the children. The Bailiff was at Home Farm and the Butler also lived on the estate.

THE GARDEN FRONT IN 1910

COPPED HALL GARDENS IN 1910
Both views courtesy of the Country Life Picture Library

Ernest Wythes had laid out an elaborate Italianate garden, on the western side of the house, set around the Causeway and with symmetrically arranged parterres, fountains, summerhouses and borders, all adorned with balustrades and obelisks, statues, wrought iron gates and topiary, which afforded a very impressive view from his new terrace. The magazine "Country Life" came and photographed it in 1910 at the height of its fame and prosperity. They also recorded the interior of the house with its ornate and expensive decoration and furnishings. The entrance hall, for instance, was panelled and contained one of the fireplaces from the Tudor mansion drawn by Sir Roger Newdigate and obviously placed in his new house by John Conyers.

THE ENTRANCE HALL IN THE MANSION IN 1910
courtesy of The Country Life Picture Library

The hall also contained the set of damask covered Roman chairs which are now at Ickworth House. The drawing room was decorated with paper imported from China, painted with Chinese scenes and furnished with lacquered pieces, the saloon had tapestries on its walls woven specially for the Hall in Paris, and the chapel, in which the household worshipped during the week, was equipped with rich ornament and panelling.

To the north of the building were placed the service areas; a range of garages to house the Rolls Royces, a stable block with the stalls for the horses made of wrought iron and teak, and of exactly the same pattern and colour as those on the Queen's estate at Sandringham and with living accommodation above for the grooms, extending around three sides of a paved courtyard and a one-storeyed dairy, with a large game larder attached, backed on to the garden, facing the laundry area. Coal chutes were situated in the basement passage which linked these areas to the house and led to large vaulted kitchens.

Ernest and Aline Wythes had three daughters, Alexandrina, Barbara and Cecilia, and the family divided their time between their various houses. They also owned a £50,000 steam yacht, one of the largest and finest in the Royal Yacht Squadron.

They were great local benefactors, especially of St. John's Church in Epping. In 1905 Ernest paid for the construction of the tower and its peal of bells and the organ, one of the finest parish organs in the country. He also donated the rood screen, above which can be seen the coat of arms of the Wythes family. The Wythes family had two pews in the front of the church, one for eight of the family and the other for six servants, the only pews ever installed there, and they also had their own entrance door. He gave money for the building of the Mechanics Institute, now known as the Hemnall Street Social Club, and contributed to other local charities. He gave the site for the Women's Institute

Hall in St. John's Road and his wife Aline was the first President of Epping Women's Institute. The Institute used to own this site on which Epping Hall is now built.

At the very young age of 27, Ernest Wythes became a magistrate on the Epping bench and served there for fifty years, being its chairman for many of those years. He was also Deputy Lieutenant of the county, High Sheriff of Essex in 1901 and appointed a C. B. E. in 1902.

He was always known as a quiet and very fair and generous man who dealt with his employees and everyone else who came into contact with him in a kindly and caring way. Sir William Addison said of him; "He did much and said little. He must have been the quietest man ever to influence for so long for good the fortunes of Epping with so few words."

THE VICTORIAN COUNTRY HOUSE

The heyday of the Victorian country house was from about 1876 to the beginning of the First World War in 1914. In that era the attitude of the upper class, living in great style in their country houses, was symbolised by the concept of "the green baize door", the door that separated the owner and his family and guests from the people who served them. The servants were supposed never to be seen, spoken to or touched by those who employed them. They used underground passages to enter the house, always used the back stairs to go up and down, cleaned the living rooms before the family rose in the morning and the bedrooms during the day, and even presented the letters to their employers on a silver salver so that their fingers would not inadvertently touch. Meals appeared on the table, fires were found miraculously lit, beds were warmed and covers turned back by invisible hands.

Society depended on rank, religion (either Church of England or Non-conformist), and a sense of duty and responsibility towards one's dependants. The estate was self-sufficient, it provided all the food and flowers, wheels for carts and shoes for horses, roads and all the other necessaries which we look to shops and specialist suppliers to provide. The walled garden, orchard, farms, stables, kennels, ice-house, laundry and game larder were all essential parts of the estate. A house the size of Copped Hall employed twenty nine indoor staff and thirty gardeners, not counting the estate workers.

Below stairs, in the servants' hall the same sense of hierarchy prevailed. The staff was divided into the "top ten" and the "bottom five". In the top ten were the butler, steward and house-keeper at the top, followed by the cook, ladies' maids and the valets who would sometimes even eat in a different place from the lower orders. The 'bottom five' were the footmen, housemaids, scullery maids and other maids with the bootboy and the daily woman at the very lowest. The person whose position was the most difficult to define was the governess, very often a gentlewoman of good education who had fallen on hard times and needed to earn her own living, lacking a father or husband to provide for her.

If the Wythes family were in residence in London, every day a cart would be sent from Copped Hall with wicker hampers containing goods from the estate; fruit, vegetables, flowers, eggs, butter, cream, poultry, milk and game. The dairy produce was from a herd of about forty pedigree Jersey cows.

There were about twenty eight staff in the house in Eaton Square and if the family were going to Epping, Mr. Wythes would hire a bus to transport the servants.

GREENHOUSES IN 1910

THE WALLED GARDEN

The walled garden at Copped Hall dates from the mid 1700s, when the walls were built, but the layout that remains today is typical of the Victorian period. Although early records of the garden are sketchy, in estate documents dated 1798 there is a listing for work done in the garden. In May that year 15 new squares of glass in the peach house and grape house were listed as costing 7s 6d (37.5p) and puttying in 27 old cucumber lights cost 6s 9d. In August, 21 squares of glass in cucumber lights cost 12s (60p). On 9 March 1799 £4 10s 6d was spent on cucumber lights, which were priced at 1s (5p) per foot.

The glasshouses in the garden are by Bolton and Paul of the Rose Lane Works in Norwich. William Bolton was a partner in a small ironmongery business in Norwich and in 1853 took on an apprentice by the name of Joseph Paul. Paul went on to become works manager and in 1864 became a partner in the business.

Within 30 years the business had grown and expanded to become one of the main suppliers of greenhouses and conservatories to royalty and owners of large estates, and to amateur gardeners with a few acres of ground.

The garden is divided into four quarters by paths, with the pond providing the central point; the quarters would have been further sub-divided by smaller paths for ease of cultivation. The 4 acres within the walls provided fruit, vegetables and flowers for the mansion, as well as the London town house, and the garden with its range of glasshouses would have been in cultivation for all 12 months of the year, supplying produce that included exotic flowers and fruit.

The area outside the walls, which was known as the slips, would also have had glasshouses, as well as cucumber pits, melon frames and compost areas, boiler houses and sheds. No space was ever wasted in the garden: the walls were used to grow fruit which was trained along wires, and the beds in front were planted with quick-growing crops such as early potatoes, spring vegetables and salad items. The heat held by the walls and the protection they provided brought the crops on much earlier than if they had been planted in open ground.

The four quarters would have been planted with main crops such as beans, peas and carrots, as well as onions and beetroot. The walled garden would also have had areas for growing flowers for cutting, and for fruit bushes such as blackcurrants, gooseberries and raspberries.

The garden was built to produce and protect crops all year round. Its slope meant that any frost rolled down the garden and away from the beds at the top of the slope – ideal for early potatoes and other frost-tender crops. The walled garden's paths were made of pebbles and hogging with a smooth surface of sand and fine gravel. They were regularly swept and kept clear of weeds. The paths were edged with blue tiles with a rope pattern top – these tops were hollow so that a metal cable could be threaded through a row of tiles to keep them straight. Behind the tile edging was a low box hedge, which prevented soil from the beds falling on the path. Much of the edging is still lying underneath the surface, as is the base of the paths.

All the glasshouses in the garden would have been purchased in kit form. The bricks would have come from local brickworks and have been built to a plan supplied with the framework. The whole structure would have been erected by the estate workers to the specification given.

Gardening was labour intensive and a strict hierarchy of staff was required for maintaining the grounds. The head gardener was in charge of the walled garden and also the other gardens surrounding the house. He would have worn a suit at all times and would have been on hand to advise and discuss the garden with the owner. He planned the planting of the crops, made the seed lists and ordered the fuel for the boilers, fertiliser, pesticides and new tools. He would have liaised with the cook on which vegetables and fruit were available and kept a diary of all the social events that were to take place throughout the year at the house. It would have been his job to hire and fire staff as well as paying the wages. He would have had his own office and, if married, would have been provided with his own house, which was usually near the walled garden.

Unmarried gardeners lived in the bothy or had a room in a larger estate house with a shared sitting room. Easy access to the garden would have been needed for the stoking of the boilers and for opening up and shutting the glasshouses in the morning and the evening. In the evenings, if a frost was due, tender plants would need to be covered, while in hot weather watering would have been carried out in the cool of the late evening rather than during the heat of the day.

THE SERVANTS

Ellen Parker was born in Wood Green, North London and attended school there until she was 14 years. Her mother died when she was 7, leaving her father with a young family. When her father married again, the stepmother had no time for the children and they were all sent away into service when they left school. Ellen took a job as maid in the house at Copped Hall in 1905. It must have seemed a long way from home for the young girl

Luckily for her she made friends with another young housemaid, Amy Amelia Wood, known as Millie, who lived in the High Street in Epping, so Ellen took to spending her free time there. In 1913 Millie's brother, Arthur, came home, discharged from army service. Arthur and Ellen fell in love and married in the Parish Church in Epping in 1914. Later Millie married Arthur's friend Albert Mead.

The two ladies, Mrs Wood and Mrs Mead, had to leave the service of Copped Hall when they married, but remained friends until Ellen's death in 1960.

George Pethurst was born in 1890 and worked as a gardener until his death in 1949. He came to Copped Hall as a journeyman with excellent references to his "sound knowledge of growing all kinds of plants, fruit and flowers indoors" as well as his character being "strictly honest, sober and of a most obliging disposition".

GEORGE PETHURST
Courtesy of Diana Thake

He arrived at Copped Hall to work in the walled garden, which by now had a large range of greenhouses equipped with ventilators and heating.

During the years 1912 to 1914 at Copped Hall he spent the first twelve months in charge of the vineries and chrysanthemums, then he changed over to the plant houses, taking charge of such flowering subjects as carnations. The chrysanthemums were propagated (on December 23rd), potted on, sprayed in fish water to prevent maggots, and fed liquid cow manure. He recorded in beautiful copperplate handwriting lists of the lily varieties that were grown and the peach trees, their dates of blooming and ripening. During this time George was an inside journeyman, adding to his knowledge under the direction of the foreman and head gardener. He lived in the bothy outside the wall of the walled garden along with all the other unmarried gardeners. In order to progress, he left Copped Hall in May 1914 for a post as inside foreman first at Reigate Priory and then at Hewell Grange.

His testimonial in May 1914 from Mr. Wythes speaks of the complete satisfaction that he gave and adds, "He is attentive to his duties and obliging in disposition".

The Head Gardener at this time was Mr Bullock, who had the reputation of being hard but fair. If one of the men slacked or stole, even a few gooseberries, he was immediately dismissed, but a young man who wanted to learn and showed aptitude was encouraged to progress. Mr. Bullock lived in the big house at the side of the walled garden. However the foreman at the time, Mr. Orman, was remembered with dread, and described as "just like Hitler to work for." There was also another foreman, Hookey Paris, who always took someone with him when he went to Epping for fear of reprisals for his treatment of the local men.

Lilian Gladys Butler, the youngest of 8 children, worked as a maid at Copped Hall from before the fire until her marriage in 1926. During her employment at Copped Hall she lived with her parents at 10 Griffin Wood Cottages. Her Father worked as a horse-keeper and her mother as a dress-maker.

Stanley Farthing worked at Copped Hall from 1915 at the age of thirteen and in his very old age remembered some interesting details of his employment and his employer, Ernest Wythes. His father was head groom there at the same time. A smart lad could get on at Copped Hall and Stanley learned the art of topiary from the Head Gardener, Mr. Bullock, and practised it in his own garden and was also taught trenching and seed planting. He remembered Ernest Wythes as a very quiet man who never spoke to the gardeners but would occasionally join in the work for a few minutes. He remembered it as a good place to work where the servants were happy and well treated, and was taught to "avoid them and wait till they go by".

The Mills family worked at Copped Hall after the fire; the father, William, was a cowman and shepherd, mother Gertrude worked in the dairy, the three boys Alfred, Harry and Alan, were gardeners and carpenters. They lived in a large, semi-detached, tied house on the estate with three large bedrooms and room to put a bed on the landing. Downstairs were front room, living/kitchen room with a scullery with a brick built copper and a kitchen range back to back with the kitchen. Outside the back door was the toilet joined on to the house (the first flush toilet they had had). Their next door neighbour was Mr. Whyte who was chauffeur to Mr. Wythes.

Henry Hatt started work as a gardener in 1921, at the age of 14, and remembered his first job, weeding the rose garden and when he had finished that being given an even worse bed to weed. (The rose garden was planted in the middle of the site of the Elizabethan house).

At Christmas time all the children on the estate under fourteen years would be invited to a party at the house with a huge Christmas tree and very nice presents for them all. They were taken to the Hall in a horse-drawn carriage. If the lake froze there would be skating parties.

The First World War began the decline of this way of life. The experience of war broke the old prejudices and certainties and men and women were no longer prepared to drudge for a very low wage. The upper classes who maintained large establishments had lost a whole generation of young men and those who returned had seen their servants in a new light having fought alongside them in ghastly conditions. The problem of getting and keeping servants was acute after the war, wages were forced up as men and women had seen the possibilities of a freer way of life for them, rather than being in service.

THE FIRE THAT DESTROYED COPPED HALL

The fire at Copped Hall occurred early in the morning on Sunday, May 6th 1917 while the family were getting ready to go to the 8am Holy Communion at St. John's Church in Epping. The cause of the fire is not known, it may have been a maid leaving a candle alight, or an electrical fault, or even a smouldering cigarette end. According to the report of the chauffeur's wife, "at first the fire was not taken seriously, and members of the household preparing for church, continued to do so", but eventually someone called the Fire Brigade.

The firemen's call bell rang in the Police Station and the men were called out by the police. Harry Woore, the Chief Officer, had to get out of bed and dress before going to the Fire Station in Station Road next to the stables where the horses that pulled the appliance were kept. The boiler in the heavy steamer was lit. There were only three men of the twelve who had been available before the war to man the pumps and hoses. These were Woore himself, Engineer Searle and Sub-Engineer Charlie Green. When they had hauled the steamer to Copped Hall, nine hundred feet of hose, in fifty foot lengths which had to be screwed together, were run out to reach the fire. Some of the lengths were already condemned but had to be put into service. They delivered a solitary jet of water. In order to save the treasures in the house, doors and windows had been opened, creating a draught which made the fire worse, but the three men did the best they could with the aid of the estate workers and servants until help arrived from another Brigade in Loughton, hauled by the horses from Saddlers at the railway station. By the end they had two thousand feet of hose in use fighting the fire, but it took until late on Monday before the wreckage of Copped Hall was deemed to be safe.

Many of the people working on the estate rushed to help save the contents and put out the flames. The gardeners and keepers helped man the hoses. Edwin Tofield who was a plumber on the estate before the War and was on leave from the Army, got his uniform scorched by the flames and had to get a letter from the Chief Constable in Epping to explain to the military authorities how he had damaged it. Mrs. Alice Grimber and Miss N. Deary were land girls at Copped Hall during World War 1, and when the alert went out Mrs. Grimble saw the glass already melting and running down the windows "like tears". Told to go to the library to save the rare books and heirlooms, Mrs. Grimble climbed from shelf to shelf throwing volumes down into baskets. They saw Mr. Wythes in his bedroom clearing out the valuables from his wall safe. Then they went to salvage in another room where they were shut in for a time as the door had jammed and they had to bang on the door for the firemen to rescue them.

Because Copped Hall was not within the Town boundary the fire was not the responsibility of Epping Council, and so Harry Woore had to pay for the use of the Steamer, the motor, the hose and the petrol used. This bill came to over £20, and he negotiated with the Insurance Company for his pay for the attendance at the fire, although we don't know how much he charged.

The family moved in to the Wood House after the fire, a Victorian house built by Mr. Wythes in 1898 for his wife's uncle, designed by Kempe and with interior designs by William Morris, and it was decided that it was more convenient to stay there.

ICKWORTH

Alice Frances Theodora Wythes (1875-1957) the grand daughter of George Wythes, and half-sister of Ernest Wythes, married Frederick, 4th Marquess of Bristol, who owned Ickworth in Suffolk. (At Ickworth she is known by her other name of Theodora). When she was born, £1,000,000 had been invested for the baby, and by the time she married this sum had grown to a staggering £18,000,000 which she used to refurbish the house and gardens at Ickworth Hall, her husband's splendid house in Suffolk. The residue was enough to endow the house so that the National Trust took it in 1956 at her death.

When Ernest and Aline Wythes moved to the Wood House they furnished it in renaissance and baroque style. The neo-classical furniture was taken to Ickworth by Alice where it suited the style of the rest of the house.The Roman chairs, which are still in place at Ickworth, were reupholstered in pink silk damask to match the pink silk curtains in the Drawing Room there, whereas at Copped Hall they were covered in red damask. A gilt console table of about the same style and date with a red marble top and a border of gilt bronze beading, also at Ickworth, was originally in the Chinese room at Copped Hall.

(By an interesting coincidence of history, Anne Poyntz, the daughter of Sir Nicholas Poyntz who was a prominent courtier under Henry VIII, became the first wife of Sir Thomas Heneage who built the Tudor Mansion at Copped Hall for her. She was an ancestress of the Hervey family, who were the Marquesses of Bristol, and owners of Ickworth Hall. A portrait of Sir Nicholas hangs at Ickworth as does a portrait of Alice Wythes.)

The estate and the gardens at Copped Hall were still kept up until the death of the couple. There were fewer employees but they lived still with a certain style. Winston Churchill's family stayed at the Wood House for two months one summer in 1924, when Churchill was standing as the candidate for the Epping Division in the general election and there were still shooting parties and picnics.

Ernest Wythes was a crack shot, reputed to be able to shoot the two birds coming towards him and then turn and shoot another two flying away from him, but he never would shoot unless he was sure of killing the birds. He employed the boys from Epping Boys School as beaters for half a crown and two sandwiches for their lunch. On the first day of the shoot they reckoned to bag

2,000 birds. There was a saying about the costs involved: "Up goes a pound, bang goes a penny, down comes half a crown". The pound was what it cost to rear a bird, the cartridge to shoot it cost a penny and they would sell it to the butcher for half a crown.

Fred Ladham remembered getting a day off school to beat when Robin Taylor was head keeper. The head keeper was responsible for buying pheasants' eggs and rearing the birds; he lived in the Piggeries on the High Road by Warren Wood and kept a herd of pigs there. Later, when he left school at 14, Fred replaced his elder brother as boy keeper, and he remembered that there was still "a massive staff". Fred was allowed to take two rabbits a week and a dozen eggs as well as ten shillings (50p) wages at first, which was raised to 25 shillings (£1.25p) by the time he was twenty five. He also received a present of a piece of beef at Christmas. The shoot had over 100 coops of 15 birds each, and about 200 birds were killed each day of the shoot. They also shot wild partridges which were common around Epping. In 1935 Fred left Copped Hall to work on another estate.

Mr. Wythes never rebuilt the mansion which was still habitable in parts, especially at the north end where the fire had done less damage. He died in 1949 and his wife two years later. A stone plaque to their memory can be found on the south wall of the Lady Chapel of St. John's Church at Epping.

Copped Hall was described by James A Brimble in his book "London's Epping Forest" published in 1950…

"On a ridge running from the woods of St. Thomas's Quarters into the middle of the park stands the great isolated shell of Copt Hall itself. It was destroyed by fire in 1917. At first glance it might be thought to be a complete mansion, but only the unburnable skeleton of walls remains. It is a gutted ruin, cluttered with debris and the unchecked growth of weeds and scrub. To the rear, now rather neglected, are the extensive ornamental Italian gardens, laid out with much grandeur, with imposing stairways, walled terraces, wrought iron gates, fountains and stone figures. There are pavilions and a derelict domed-roof conservatory, containing even now beautiful camellias. On the terrace a stone figure of Justice, with upheld scales, stands on its pedestal. One pan of the scales hangs broken and swinging, and clanks and clangs in the wind. Everywhere there is decay and desolation. On a moonlight night, Copped Hall has an eerie and haunted atmosphere.......

But the glory of Copt Hall is no more. Apart from a few old trees, all its associations with the Forest and its past and colourful history have disappeared. There are colonies of rooks in the trees around. Jackdaws nest and quarrel within and on top of the high roofless walls. Their undisputed possession of the uninhabitable shell – their endless monotonous chatter and cawing – only seems to emphasise the finality of the story".

CHAPTER FOUR
DESTRUCTION AND PRESERVATION

In 1952 the whole estate, consisting of nearly 4,000 acres with ten tenanted farms, was sold. The purchaser was the Talbot Trust, a family land-owning trust of the Fletchers of Margam in Wales, the lifetime beneficiary of which was John Theodore Talbot Fletcher, who lived in Toot Hill and later in Theydon Place, Epping, where he died in 1995. During the fifties, everything of value in and around the mansion was sold or removed.

THE WEST FRONT OF COPPED HALL IN 1999
by W. R. Conolly

The great staircases, garden stonework and statuary were all dispersed. The massive iron gates and railings were shipped to America. The conservatory was dynamited, allegedly as part of an army exercise. The gardens became infested with weeds and

75

sycamores which choked and killed off many of the specimen trees and shrubs. Vandalism was rife and added to the decay of the roofless property. The ruined building was used to grow mushrooms, and pigs and chickens were reared there.

PLANS FOR DEVELOPMENT

The building of the M25 Motorway through the parkland drew the attention of property developers to the value of the site. The first planning application was submitted by Sherfield Developments in 1986. The application was for the building of a vast commercial office block enveloping the mansion with parking facilities for hundreds of vehicles. The Epping Society and the Upshire Village Preservation Society, enthusiastically supported by Alan Cox, an architect with a passion for the protection of the integrity of Copped Hall, were roused to fight against the planning application. A small committee chaired by Lady Patricia Gibberd and including representatives from the Friends of Epping Forest was formed as the Friends of Copped Hall. This group, by emphasising the importance of Copped Hall as a much loved building with important historical connections within the Green Belt, managed to persuade the Council to refuse the application.

The mansion, ancillary buildings, lodges and surrounding gardens were then sold to another developer who drew up plans for a large hotel with extra buildings in the gardens and a golf course. Again this was successfully opposed. The property was again sold on, the developer having made a handsome profit without spending a penny on the protection of the mansion. The owner was now Cambridgeshire Property Developments Ltd. which was caught in the property crash of the early 1990's and collapsed in 1992. The Royal Trust Bank of Canada now held a legal charge on the property through their property arm, Gentra Ltd.

The Conservators of Epping Forest, who had kept a watchful eye on proceedings, now stepped in and bought 785 acres of land surrounding the mansion from the Copped Hall Estate. This would not only serve as "buffer land" for Epping Forest but also preclude any golf course plans.

THE COPPED HALL TRUST

The Royal Trust Bank, aware of the problems of corporate ownership of a listed building, was persuaded that a properly constituted Charitable Trust would be the ideal owners of Copped Hall. Accordingly the Copped Hall Trust was immediately set up. Its first trustees were Lady Pat Gibberd, Ann Bartlett, Alan Cox and Denys Favre. The Trust's specialist charity solicitors obtained charitable status on 15th December 1993.

The daunting task now began to find the thousands of pounds required to buy the property. Banks were either not interested or would not lend the money for such a complex proposal. After much searching, Alan Cox found Maria Bjornson, the stage designer for many international musicals and operas, who came to Copped Hall and was prepared to lend half of the finance. This confidence in the project encouraged the Architectural Heritage Fund to lend the other half. The loans came with stringent conditions but at the very last moment, just before the final deadline, the legal complications were sorted out and the Trust became the owners of Copped Hall.

To pay off the loans and interest, parts of the stable block and other outhouses were sold on long leases with covenants to protect the integrity of the site. Sensitive restoration has converted these buildings at the north end of the site to attractive dwellings.

With the freehold now held by a Charitable Trust the criteria for future development was established. The aim was to restore the interior of the mansion to its mid-eighteenth century form; there would be no new building or sale of any part of the mansion; no regular mass car parking in the vicinity of the mansion would be allowed; and Copped Hall would be used to produce an understanding of the place and its historical and educational importance.

The first few years were very worrying times financially for the members of the Trust but with the aid of several very generous local people who stepped in with offers of low interest loans to tide the Trust over, somehow the project weathered the early storms and continued to fight to preserve what was left of the buildings and rescue the gardens from further destruction by weed growth and vandalism.

In 1996 the Racquets Court was restored, with the help of a grant from Epping Forest District Council. It can now be used for meetings and exhibitions. In 1998 the Friends of the Copped Hall Trust was set up and began to flourish with the aim of supporting the Trust in its activities by financial and practical help.

The Friends have been one of the most valuable resources the Trust has; they raise funds, organise tours of the grounds, visit groups to recount the history of the house and assist the Trust with other educational and social activities. A large number work in the gardens, clearing and planting, meeting mainly on Sunday mornings, but some enjoy coming in during the week to work on a special project.

The concerts, plays, music and other events held at Copped Hall have had a dual function; they have added to the revenue that the

Trust generates by its activities and have brought new people to the Hall to enjoy its facilities and learn more about the project. One of the first events, held in the gardens, was a production of "Midsummer Night's Dream" which proved so popular that ever since an annual Shakespeare play in the open air in various parts of the gardens has been held. Musical evenings have also proved very popular, ranging from classical piano playing to traditional jazz and from Christmas carols to operatic arias. Adult study days and school groups, usually with a historical theme, can now be held in the wing of the mansion and exhibitions of art and history staged in the multi-purpose rooms have also been a continuing success. These events are enhanced by the home-made refreshments that our team of caterers provide.

The walled garden was returned to the Copped Hall Trust in 1999. When the old wooden door in the wall at the top of the garden was opened there was just a tangled mass of brambles, self-sown trees and weeds. The glasshouses at the bottom of the garden were barely visible, the pond was almost completely full of reed mace, with just a small area of water in the deepest part, and most of the pear tree walk was in ruins with the hoops lying on the ground or missing.

Looking back on what has happened to the garden since work started gives an idea of how the work has progressed. Between the years 1999 and 2005 all the brambles and shrubs have been cleared, as have the glasshouses and now these are used for growing vegetables. Further beds have been dug and trees planted against the west wall at the bottom of the garden and now a considerable amount of ground is under cultivation. The central pond has been cleared back to its original size and now provides a focal point at the end of the pear tree walk.

GREENHOUSES IN 2000
By J.A.Keith ARPS

The walled garden team works hard and produces as much vegetables and fruit as possible, the sale of which provides much needed money to enable further restoration. In 2005 an asparagus bed was planted and it will provide more saleable produce. Part of the garden is being used for growing box for topiary, an arrangement which provides box hedging every year to use to edge the new beds.

In 2001, funds became available to start on the house and scaffolding was erected to enable the roof structure to be reinstated so that the chimneys, which were in a rather precarious state, could be made safer. Once the scaffolding was up, it was possible to put in girders and begin re-roofing the building, with at least a temporary roof that would further safeguard the house and make it possible to admit visitors to the entrance hall, the basements and the link to the stable block, where the Trust still own the original stables with the living accommodation above being sold leasehold. The Trust began to organise tours of the mansion in 2003 and this is an ever-expanding part of the work as more sections of the house are being roofed and floored as funds become available.

Visitors were taken upstairs to see Lady Henrietta's bedroom and get a view of the Entrance Hall from above in 2005 and in 2006 parts of the wing were designated for use by the educational section of the project, with study groups and school parties finding this part of the house a useful asset.

DAVE KARASKAS AND THE CHIMNEYS
by Peter Dalton

A visit by His Royal Highness the Prince of Wales on 27th April 2004 provided a further royal connection in the long history of Copped Hall. The visit was an acknowledgement of and encouragement for all the volunteers whose hard work and dedication make the restoration of Copped Hall and its gardens such a successful project.

HRH THE PRINCE OF WALES
with Denys Favre, Chairman of the Trust

THE ACQUISITION FUND

Another project of the Trust is acquiring artefacts that have associations with the Hall. A special Fund has been set up for the purpose, using funds that are specifically donated. The first was a hall seat that was made specially for Copped Hall carrying the initials JC, those of the second John Conyers. Various pictures, notably eleven botanical paintings by Matilda Conyers, the daughter of the first John Conyers and a drawing by Juliana Conyers, have been donated or bought. A number of books which used to be in the Conyers' library and which carry the Conyers bookplate were purchased. Various items of stone-work have been returned to the gardens. Twelve interesting grape storage bottles, patented by Copped Hall and made by Wood and Son will eventually be displayed in the kitchens along with a quantity of copper pots and pans and other relevant kitchen articles donated by various Friends.

The latest acquisition and one that has aroused a great deal of interest is the return of a 20 horse-power Rolls-Royce owned by Mrs Wythes in 1929, and sold before her death to her chauffeur so that he could set up a car hire business in Epping. In 1978 a Dr. Jago meticulously restored the car and on his death in 2005 the car was offered back to Copped Hall by his widow.

Another very important aspect of the work at Copped Hall is the archaeological investigations undertaken by West Essex Archaeological Group who continued the search for the remains of the medieval and Elizabethan foundations. Subsequently a systematic and scholarly investigation is ongoing every summer by students under the direction of Dr. Neil Faulkner and Tina Holloway acting with the support of WEAG, which is uncovering, recording and dating the various layers of the history under our feet.

ARCHAEOLOGICAL DIG
By Sylvia Keith ARPS

Many finds have come to light, ranging from Roman pottery and medieval tiles to nineteenth century pipes and twentieth century sanitary ware. This work is a valuable addition to our knowledge and also part of the educational aims of the whole project. It has already confirmed the fact that the medieval hall was incorporated into the larger Tudor building created by Sir Thomas Heneage and is beginning to confirm the area of the Tudor mansion itself.

PLANS FOR THE FUTURE

The Trust has a three pronged policy for Copped Hall. The first objective is to preserve what it owns, by preventing development which would jeopardise the integrity of the site and by making sure that the fabric of the building and gardens is cleared of weed growth, protected from vandals and does not deteriorate further. A second and important aim is to educate the public, both schoolchildren and adults, in the history and importance of the place. This is being achieved by guided tours, exhibitions and lectures, and bringing out pamphlets and books on the subject. Lastly the plan is to restore and repair, where it is possible, the historic aspects of the Hall and garden, especially to restore the house as it was in 1758, keeping in mind the multi-layered nature of the history of this fascinating site. Ultimately the mansion will be used for a variety of community purposes.

So for Copped Hall and its gardens the twentieth century may be summarized as splendour, decay and resurrection and we expect it to play an important if very different role in the social history of the twenty-first century.